STUDENT'S BOOK 1

SERIES EDITORS
Joan Kang Shin and
JoAnn (Jodi) Crandall

AUTHORS
Lesley Koustaff and
Susan Rivers

T0349567

The Alphabet

1 **Look and listen.** Say. TR: 0.1

Aa apple

Bb baby

Cc cat

Gg goat

Hh hand

Ii ice cream

Mm monkey

Nn nine

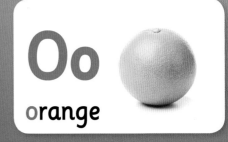
Oo orange

Ss sock

Tt turtle

Uu umbrella

Yy yellow

Zz zebra

Dd dog

Ee egg

Ff fish

Jj jacket

Kk kite

Ll lamp

Pp pencil

Qq queen

Rr robot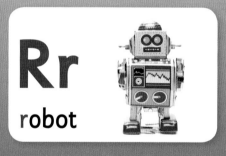

Vv vegetables

Ww water

Xx fox

a b c d e f g h i j k l m n o p q r s t u v w x y z

apple

baby

cat

a b c **d** e **f** g h i j k l m n o p q r s t u v w x y z

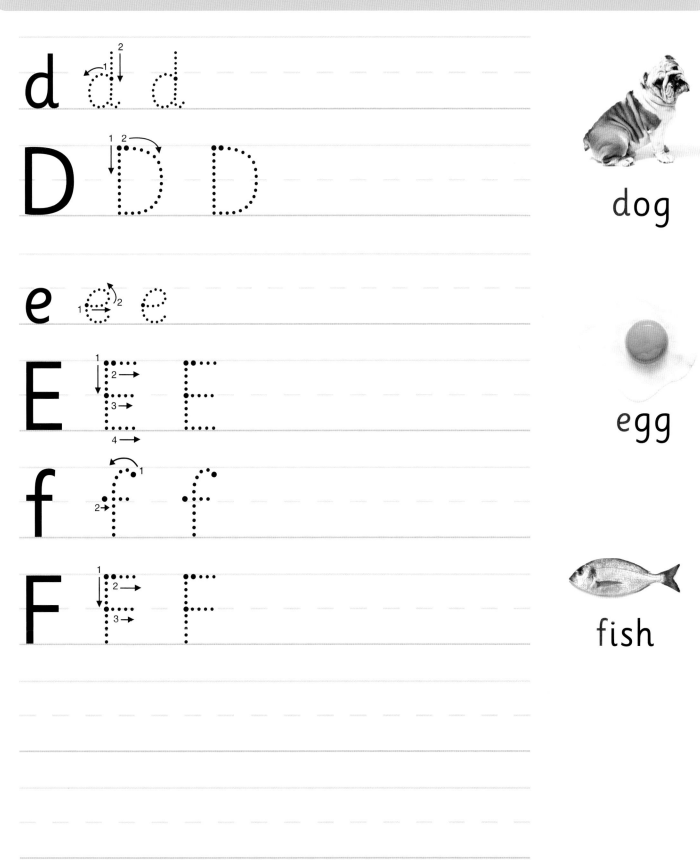

d

D

e

E

f

F

dog

egg

fish

a b c d e f **g** **h** **i** j k l m n o p q r s t u v w x y z

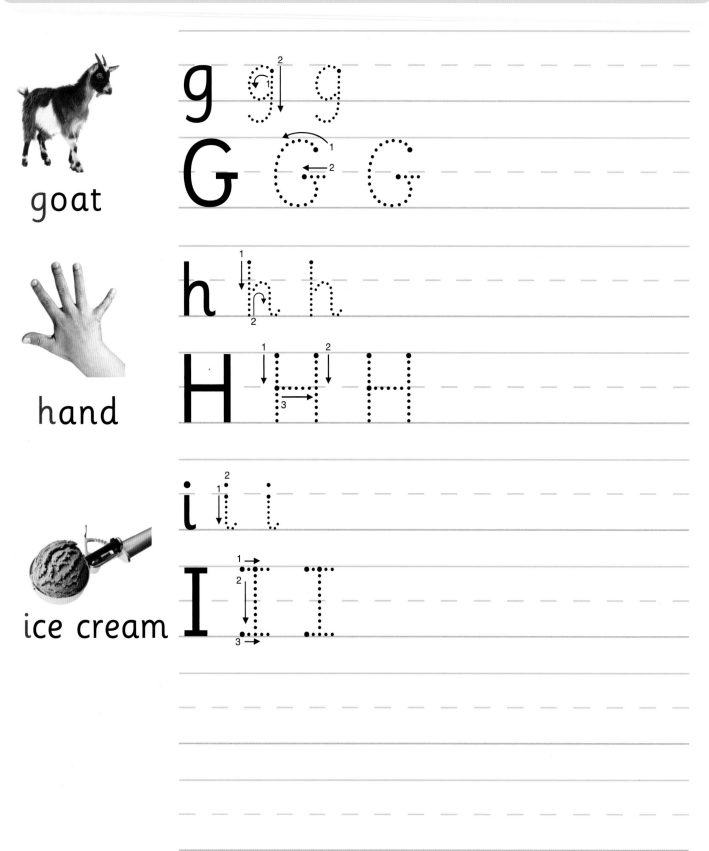

goat

hand

ice cream

Listen and say. Write. TR: 0.5

a b c d e f g h i j **k** l m n o p q r s t u v w x y z

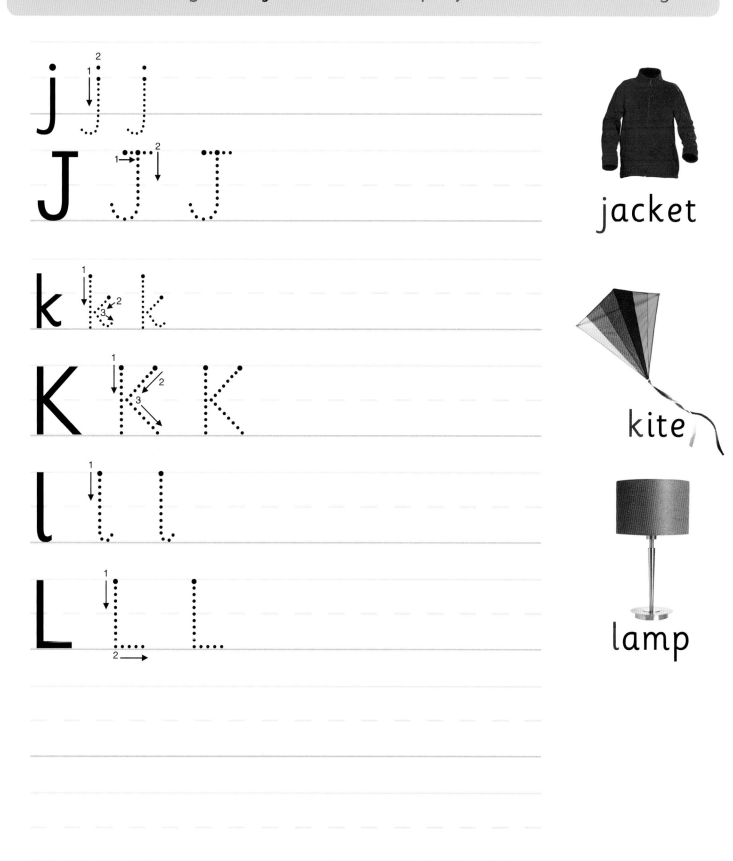

j

J

k

K

l

L

jacket

kite

lamp

a b c d e f g h i j k l **m n o** p q r s t u v w x y z

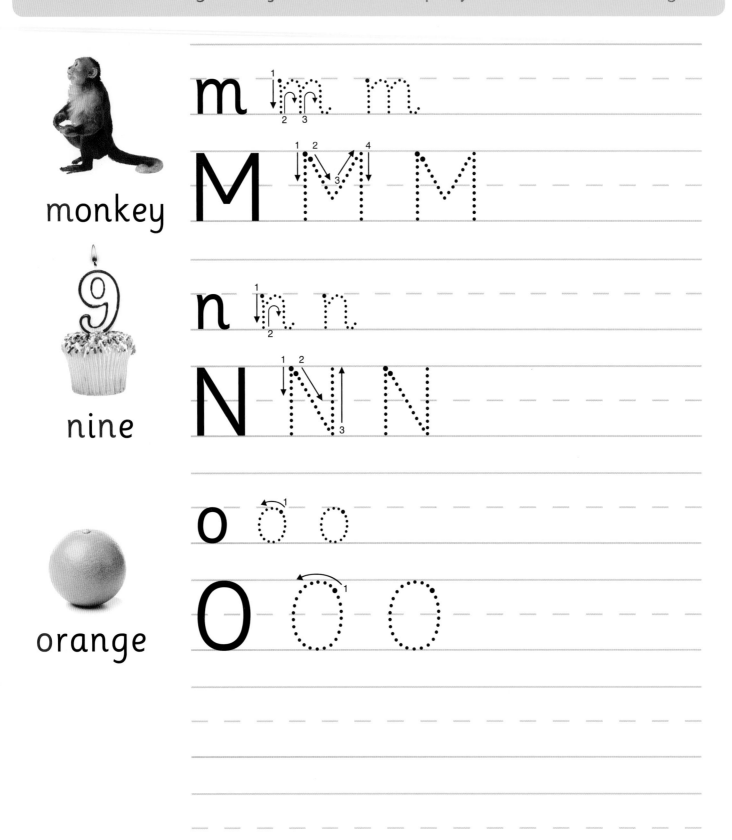

monkey

nine

orange

a b c d e f g h i j k l m n o **p** q r s t u v w x y z

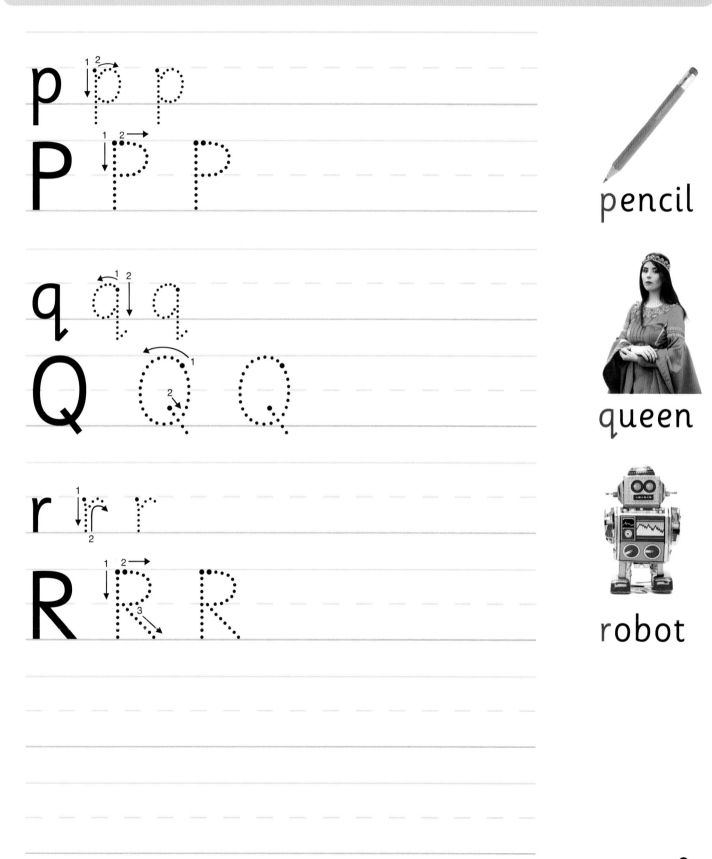

pencil

queen

robot

a b c d e f g h i j k l m n o p q r **s t** u **v** w x y z

sock

turtle

umbrella

vegetables

a b c d e f g h i j k l m n o p q r s t u v **w** x y z

w

W

x

X

y

Y

z

Z

water

fox

yellow

zebra

11

(1) Listen. Then listen and repeat. TR: 1.1 and 1.2

1.

pen

2.

paint

3.

map

4.

top

5.

happy

(2) Trace and say.

(3) Is p at the beginning, in the middle or at the end? Listen and repeat. Tick. ✓ TR: 1.3

1.

○ ○ ○

2.

○ ○ ○

3.

○ ○ ○

4.

○ ○ ○

(4) Can you hear p? Listen and circle *Yes* or *No*. TR: 1.4

1. Yes No   2. Yes No   3. Yes No   4. Yes No

5 **Listen.** Then listen and repeat. TR: 1.5 and 1.6

Bb

1. book

2. ball

3. cub

4. robot

5. rainbow

6 **Trace and say.**

7 **Is b at the beginning, in the middle or at the end?**
Listen and repeat. Tick. ✓ TR: 1.7

1. ○ ○ ○   2. ○ ○ ○   3. ○ ○ ○   4. ○ ○ ○

8 **Can you hear p or b?** Listen and write *p* or *b*. TR: 1.8

1. _____   2. _____   3. _____   4. _____

9 **Listen.** Then listen and repeat. TR: 1.9 and 1.10

1.

ten

2.

table

3.

sit

4.

goat

5.

fourteen

10 **Trace and say.**

11 **Is t at the beginning, in the middle or at the end?**
Listen and repeat. Tick. ✔ TR: 1.11

1.

○ ○ ○

2.
○ ○ ○

3.
○ ○ ○

4.
○ ○ ○

12 **Can you hear t?** Listen and (circle) *Yes* or *No*. TR: 1.12

1. Yes No   2. Yes No   3. Yes No   4. Yes No

14

13 **Listen.** Then listen and repeat. TR: 1.13 and 1.14

Dd

1.

2.

d esk   d oor

3.

4.

5.

boar d   sa d   noo d les

14 **Trace and say.**

15 **Is d at the beginning, in the middle or at the end?**
Listen and repeat. Tick.  TR: 1.15

1.

2.

3.

4.

○ ○ ○   ○ ○ ○   ○ ○ ○   ○ ○ ○

16 **Can you hear t or d?** Listen and write *t* or *d*. TR: 1.16

1. _____   2. _____   3. _____   4. _____

17 **Look, say and circle.** Use red, blue, green and black.

○ p   ○ b   ○ t   ○ d

18 **Listen.** Then listen and chant. TR: 1.17

Sounds and letters. Letters and sounds.
Clap your hands and turn around.

Pens and paper, p p p.
Book and ball, b b b.
Toys and tablet, t t t.
Desk and window, d d d.

Sounds and letters. Letters and sounds.
Clap your hands and turn around.

Listen. Then listen and repeat. TR: 1.18 and 1.19

Bella's First Day at School

It's Bella's first day at school. She puts paper, books, pencils and a map in her bag.

Poor Bella! Her bag is big. She's tired!

Books on your desks, please.

Yes, Mrs Todd.

My puzzle, my teddy bear, my doll and my robot ... and here's my book!

20 **Which sound can you hear?** Listen and (circle).
Then go to page 78. TR: 1.20

| **1** t | **2** b | **3** b | **4** d |
| **1** d | **2** t | **3** p | **4** p |

1 Listen. Then listen and repeat. TR: 2.1 and 2.2

Ss

1.

2.

sun

sky

3.

4.

5.

grass   classroom   desk

2 Trace and say.

3 Is s at the beginning, in the middle or at the end?
Listen and repeat. Tick. ✔ TR: 2.3

1.

2.

3.

4.

○ ○ ○   ○ ○ ○   ○ ○ ○   ○ ○ ○

4 Can you hear s? Listen and circle *Yes* or *No*. TR: 2.4

1. Yes No   2. Yes No   3. Yes No   4. Yes No

5 Listen. Then listen and repeat. TR: 2.5 and 2.6

Zz

1.
zebra

2.
zero

3.
```
Name: _____
Date: _____

1.  2 + 2 = _____
2.  3 + 1 = _____
3.  2 + 1 = _____
```
quiz

4.
lizard

5.
puzzle

6 Trace and say.

7 Is z at the beginning, in the middle or at the end?
Listen and repeat. Tick. ✔ TR: 2.7

1.  ◯ ◯ ◯

2. ◯ ◯ ◯

3.
```
Name: _____
Date: _____

1.  3 + 1 = ___
2.  3 − 1 = ___
    1 + 2 =
```
◯ ◯ ◯

4. ◯ ◯ ◯

8 Can you hear s or z? Listen and write s or z. TR: 2.8

1. _____   2. _____   3. _____   4. _____

9 **Listen.** Then listen and repeat. TR: 2.9 and 2.10

1.
2.

mountain   moon

3.
4.
5.

arm   bedroom   family

10 **Trace and say.**

11 **Is m at the beginning, in the middle or at the end?**
Listen and repeat. Tick. ✓ TR: 2.11

1.  ○ ○ ○
2.  ○ ○ ○
3.  ○ ○ ○
4.  ○ ○ ○

12 **Can you hear m?** Listen and (circle) *Yes* or *No.* TR: 2.12

1. Yes No   2. Yes No   3. Yes No   4. Yes No

13 **Listen.** Then listen and repeat. TR: 2.13 and 2.14

Nn

1.

n est

2.

n ose

3.

lion

4.

balloon

5.

rainbow

14 **Trace and say.**

15 **Is n at the beginning, in the middle or at the end?**
Listen and repeat. Tick. ✓ TR: 2.15

1.

○ ○ ○

2.

○ ○ ○

3.

○ ○ ○

4.

○ ○ ○

16 **Can you hear m or n?** Listen and write *m* or *n*. TR: 2.16

1. _____   2. _____   3. _____   4. _____

17 **Follow the path to the sound at the beginning of the word.**

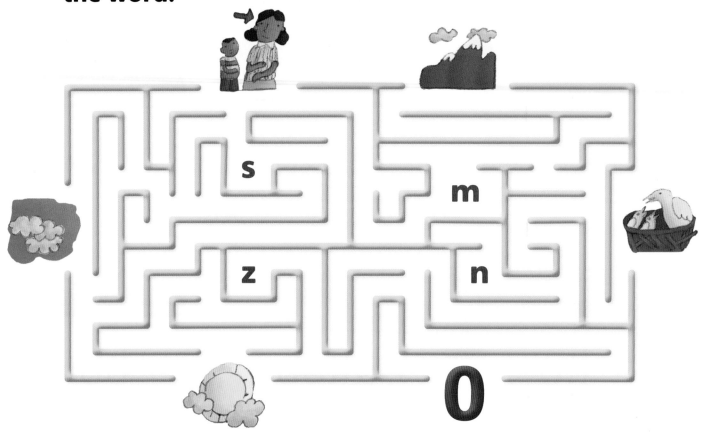

18 **Listen.** Then listen and chant. TR: 2.17

Time to chant for you and me!
Let's chant together 1, 2, 3.

Moon over the mountain, m m m.
Lions in the den, n n n.
Sunset in the sky, s s s.
Zebras in the zoo, z z z.

Let's chant together 1, 2, 3.
This is fun for you and me!

19 **Listen.** Then listen and repeat. TR: 2.18 and 2.19

Nature Day

The moon is over the mountain. The lion is in the den.

The sun is in the sky. The zebra is in the grass.

The rainbow is in the sky. The panda is on the mountain.

The seal is in the sea. The lizard is on me!

20 **Which sound can you hear?** Listen and (circle.) Then go to page 78. TR: 2.20

1 s	**2** n	**3** m	**4** m
1 z	**2** z	**3** s	**4** n

1 **Listen.** Then listen and repeat. TR: 3.1 and 3.2

Ff

1.

family

2.

farm

3.

leaf

4.

father

5.

muffin

2 **Trace and say.**

3 **Is f at the beginning, in the middle or at the end?**
Listen and repeat. Tick. ✔ TR: 3.3

1.
○ ○ ○

2.
○ ○ ○

3.
○ ○ ○

4.
○ ○ ○

4 **Can you hear f?** Listen and circle Yes or No. TR: 3.4

1. Yes No   2. Yes No   3. Yes No   4. Yes No

5 **Listen.** Then listen and repeat. TR: 3.5 and 3.6

Vv

1.
van

2.
visit

3.
love

4.
glove

5.
river

6 **Trace and say.**

7 **Is v at the beginning, in the middle or at the end?**
Listen and repeat. Tick. ✔ TR: 3.7

1.
○ ○ ○

2.
○ ○ ○

3.
○ ○ ○

4.
○ ○ ○

8 **Can you hear f or v?** Listen and write *f* or *v*. TR: 3.8

1.  _____   2. _____   3. _____   4. _____

9 **Listen.** Then listen and repeat. TR: 3.9 and 3.10

1.

2.

girl   goat

3.

4.

5.

egg   big   kangaroo

10 **Trace and say.**

11 **Is g at the beginning, in the middle or at the end?**
Listen and repeat. Tick. ✔ TR: 3.11

1.    2.    3.    4.

○ ○ ○   ○ ○ ○   ○ ○ ○   ○ ○ ○

12 **Can you hear g?** Listen and circle Yes or No. TR: 3.12

1. Yes No   2. Yes No   3. Yes No   4. Yes No

13 **Listen.** Then listen and repeat. TR: 3.13 and 3.14

1.

lion

2.

lemon

3.

pencil

4.

small

5.

balloon

14 **Trace and say.**

15 **Is l at the beginning, in the middle or at the end?**
Listen and repeat. Tick. ✔ TR: 3.15

1.

◯ ◯ ◯

2.

◯ ◯ ◯

3.

◯ ◯ ◯

4.

◯ ◯ ◯

16 **Can you hear g or l?** Listen and write g or l. TR: 3.16

1. _____ 2. _____ 3. _____ 4. _____

17 **Find the three words in a row.** Then listen and repeat.
Check your answers. TR: 3.17

I. f, v, g or l at the
   beginning

2. f, v, g or l at the end

18 **Listen.** Then listen and chant. TR: 3.18

Come on, girls,
Come on, boys.
Clap your hands
and make some noise!

Fun with my family, f f f.
Daddy drives the van, v v v.
Big burgers taste good, g g g.
We have lunch by the lake, l l l.

Come on, girls,
Come on, boys.
Clap your hands
and make some noise!

19 **Listen.** Then listen and repeat. TR: 3.19 and 3.20

Fun at the Farm

The family visits Grandpa's farm. The girls love to go there.

Look, lambs! Gabi gives the small lamb some lettuce. Lambs love food.

Look, goats! Lidia feeds the little goat some vegetables. Goats are funny.

The girls love the farm. Their father doesn't like the farm. He wants to get in the van and go home!

Goodbye, Grandpa!

20 **Which sound can you hear?** Listen and circle.
Then go to page 78. TR: 3.21

1 f	**2** v	**3** g	**4** g
1 l	**2** f	**3** l	**4** v

Review

Start

___oon

___amily

___an

___ion

___en

ma___

___un

Move forwards I space.

e___

___irl

li___ard

Move back 1 space.

ri__er

Finish

__est

__ky

__able

__ook

__ebra

__lea__

si__

__esk

1 **Work in pairs.** Write the letters.

2 **Play the game.** Say the letter, sound and word.

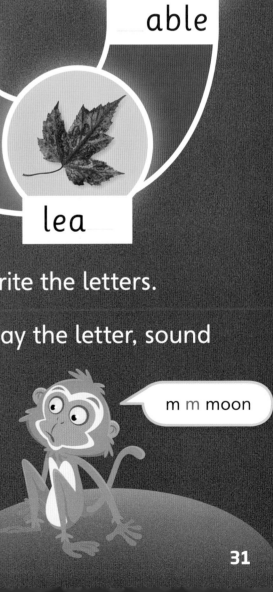

m m moon

Heads: Move 1 space.

Tails: Move 2 spaces.

1 **Listen.** Then listen and repeat. TR: 4.1 and 4.2

Aa

1.

2.

apple   cap

3.

4.

5.

pan   bag   lamp

2 **Trace and say.**

3 **Can you hear a?** Listen and (circle) *Yes* or *No.* TR: 4.3

1. Yes No   2. Yes No   3. Yes No   4. Yes No

4 **Can you hear the word with a one or two times?**
Listen and (circle) *1* or *2.* TR: 4.4

1.

2.

3.

4.

1 2   1 2   1 2   1 2

5 Listen. Then listen and repeat. TR: 4.5 and 4.6

Ee

1.

egg

2.

ten

3.

bed

4.

desk

5.

shelf

6 Trace and say.

7 Can you hear e? Listen and (circle) Yes or No. TR: 4.7

1. Yes No   2. Yes No   3. Yes No   4. Yes No

8 Can you hear a or e? Listen and write a or e. TR: 4.8

1.    2.    3.    4.

n ck   b t   w b   p n

9 **Listen.** Then listen and repeat. TR: 4.9 and 4.10

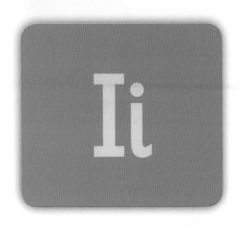

1.

in

2.

big

3.

sit

4.

fish

5.

kitchen

10 **Trace and say.**

11 **Can you hear i?** Listen and (circle) *Yes* or *No*. TR: 4.11

l. Yes No   2. Yes No   3. Yes No   4. Yes No

12 **Can you hear the word with i one or two times?**
Listen and (circle) *l* or *2*. TR: 4.12

1.

2.

3.

4.

   l   2   l   2   l   2   l   2

13 Listen. Then listen and repeat. TR: 4.13 and 4.14

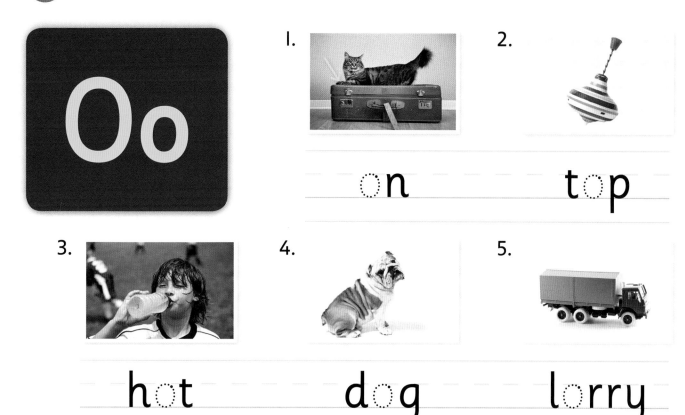

Oo

1. on

2. top

3. hot

4. dog

5. lorry

14 Trace and say.

15 Can you hear o? Listen and circle Yes or No. TR: 4.15

1. Yes No   2. Yes No   3. Yes No   4. Yes No

16 Can you hear i or o? Listen and write i or o. TR: 4.16

1. m_lk   2. s_ck   3. p_t   4. s_x

17 **Look, say and circle.** Use red, blue, green and black.

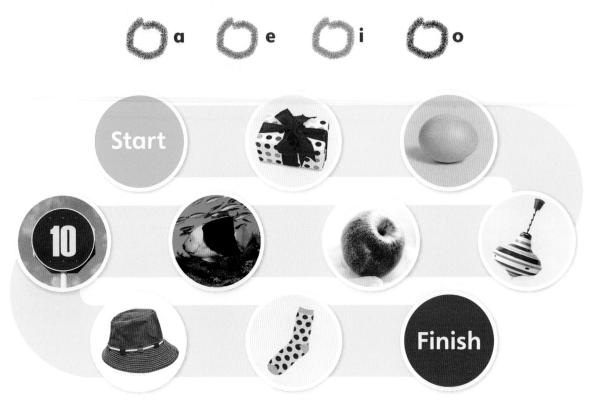

18 **Listen.** Then listen and chant. TR: 4.17

Sounds and letters.
Letters and sounds.
Clap your hands
and turn around.

Bag in the bathroom, a a a.
Egg in the bedroom, e e e.
Fish in the kitchen, i i i.
Sock in the pot, o o o.

Sounds and letters.
Letters and sounds.
Clap your hands
and turn around.

19 **Listen.** Then listen and repeat. TR: 4.18 and 4.19

Eddy's Cap

Where's Eddy's cap? He looks on his bed and in his desk. It isn't there.

Eddy looks in his bag. He looks under the lamp by his dad.

It isn't here.

Eddy looks in the pots and pans in the kitchen. He looks on the shelf, too. It isn't there.

Look! Ziggy the dog has got my cap!

20 **Which sound can you hear?** Listen and circle. Then go to page 78. TR: 4.20

| **1** a | **2** e | **3** i | **4** i |
| **1** o | **2** a | **3** o | **4** a |

1 **Listen.** Then listen and repeat. TR: 5.1 and 5.2

Uu

1.

up

2.

run

3.

bus

4.

duck

5.

lunch

2 **Trace and say.**

3 **Can you hear u?** Listen and circle *Yes* or *No*. TR: 5.3

1. Yes No   2. Yes No   3. Yes No   4. Yes No

4 **Can you hear the word with u one or two times?**
Listen and circle *1* or *2*. TR: 5.4

1.

1 2

2.

1 2

3.

1 2

4.

1 2

5 **Listen.** Then listen and repeat. TR: 5.5 and 5.6

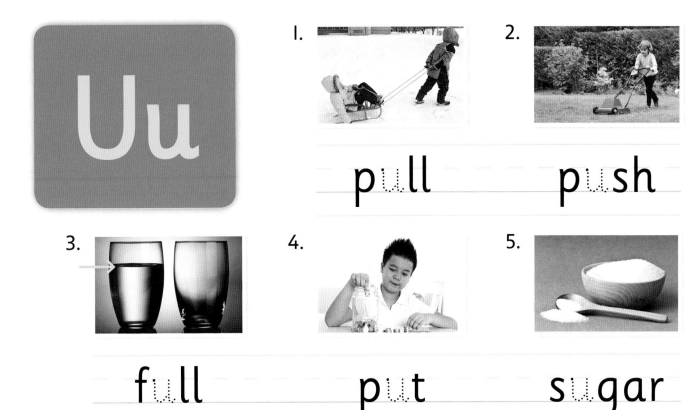

Uu

1. pull

2. push

3. full

4. put

5. sugar

6 **Trace and say.**

7 **Can you hear u?** Listen and (circle) *Yes* or *No*. TR: 5.7

1. Yes No   2. Yes No   3. Yes No   4. Yes No

8 **Can you hear u as in *sun* or u as in *put*?** Listen and (circle) green or blue. TR: 5.8

1.    2.    3.    4.

9 **Listen.** Then listen and repeat. TR: 5.9 and 5.10

1.

2.

yawn   young

3.

4.

5.

yell   yoghurt   yellow

10 **Trace and say.**

11 **Can you hear y?** Listen and (circle) Yes or No. TR: 5.11

1. Yes No   2. Yes No   3. Yes No   4. Yes No

12 **Can you hear the word with y one or two times?**
Listen and (circle) 1 or 2. TR: 5.12

1.

2.

3.

4.

1 2   1 2   1 2   1 2

13 **Listen.** Then listen and repeat. **TR: 5.13 and 5.14**

1.

fifty

2.

sleepy

3.

4.

5.

happy   sunny   baby

14 **Trace and say.**

15 **Can you hear y?** Listen and (circle) Yes or No. **TR: 5.15**

1. Yes No   2. Yes No   3. Yes No   4. Yes No

16 **Can you hear y as in *yellow* or y as in *baby*?**
Listen and (circle) green or blue. **TR: 5.16**

1.

2.

3.

4.

17 Follow the path to the pictures with the same sound.

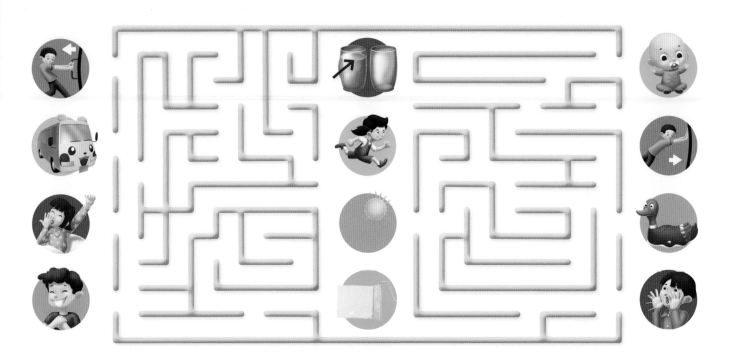

18 **Listen.** Then listen and chant. TR: 5.17

Time to chant for you and me!
Let's chant together 1, 2, 3.

Jumping in puddles, u u u.
Pushing and pulling, u u u.
Yummy, yummy yoghurt, y y y.
Very messy day, y y y.

Let's chant together 1, 2, 3.
This is fun for you and me!

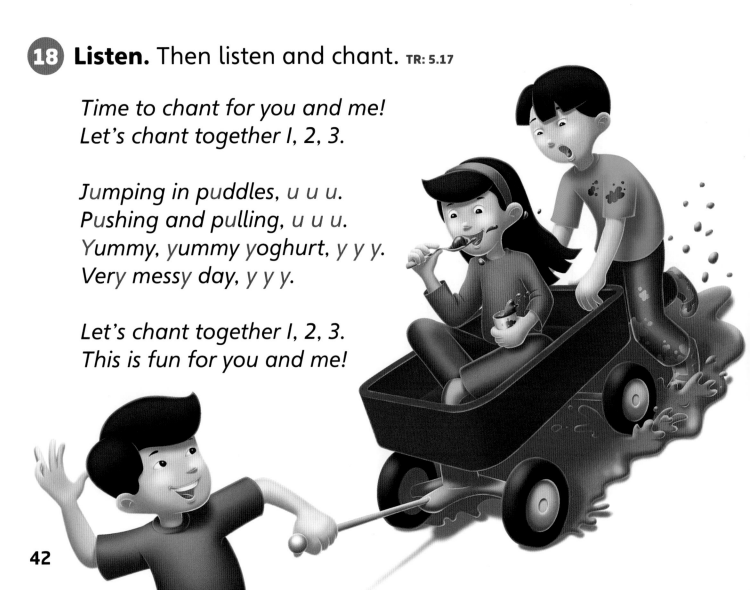

19 **Listen.** Then listen and repeat. TR: 5.18 and 5.19

Yoko Gets Dressed

Yoko! It's seven fifty! Get up! You're late.

Yoko yawns.

Yoko puts on her shirt.
She puts on her yellow hat.
She's sleepy!

Hurry up, Yoko! Here's your lunch. Run to the bus!

Oh, yummy! Strawberry yoghurt! Thank you, Mum!

The bus arrives. Yoko's yellow hat falls off.

Oh, no! My pyjamas!

20 **Which sound can you hear?** Listen and circle. Then go to page 79. TR: 5.20

1 u as in *full*	**2** u as in *sugar*	**3** y as in *yawn*	**4** y as in *yell*
1 u as in *nut*	**2** y as in *fifty*	**3** u as in *lunch*	**4** y as in *puppy*

1 **Listen.** Then listen and repeat. TR: 6.1 and 6.2

Cc

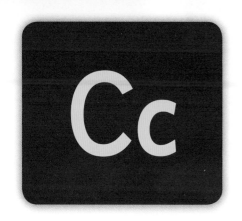

1.

2.

cat   car

3.

4.

5.

cup   cake   colour

2 **Trace and say.**

3 **Can you hear c?** Listen and (circle) Yes or No. TR: 6.3

1. Yes No   2. Yes No   3. Yes No   4. Yes No

4 **Can you hear the word with c one or two times?**
Listen and (circle) 1 or 2. TR: 6.4

1.    2.    3.    4.

1 2   1 2   1 2   1 2

5 **Listen.** Then listen and repeat. TR: 6.5 and 6.6

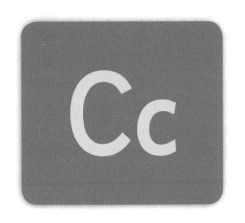

1.

circle

2.

city

3.

face

4.

juice

5.
pencil

6 **Trace and say.**

7 **Is c at the beginning, in the middle or at the end?** Listen and repeat. Tick. ✔ TR: 6.7

1.

○ ○ ○

2.

○ ○ ○

3.

○ ○ ○

4.

○ ○ ○

8 **Can you hear c as in *cat* or c as in *circle*?** Listen and (circle) green or blue. TR: 6.8

1. cereal   2. picnic   3. cart   4. mice

45

9 **Listen.** Then listen and repeat. TR: 6.9 and 6.10

Kk

1.
king

2.
kite

3.
book

4.
walk

5.
blanket

10 **Trace and say.**

11 **Is k at the beginning, in the middle or at the end?**
Listen and repeat. Tick. ✓ TR: 6.11

1.
○ ○ ○

2.
○ ○ ○

3.
○ ○ ○

4.
○ ○ ○

12 **Can you hear k?** Listen and ⬭circle⬭ Yes or No. TR: 6.12

1. Yes No   2. Yes No   3. Yes No   4. Yes No

13 **Listen.** Then listen and repeat. TR: 6.13 and 6.14

1.

fox

2.

box

3.

six

4.

mix

5.

taxi

14 **Trace and say.**

15 **Can you hear x?** Listen and circle *Yes* or *No*. TR: 6.15

1. Yes No   2. Yes No   3. Yes No   4. Yes No

16 **Can you hear k or x?** Listen and write *k* or *x*. TR: 6.16

1.    2.   3.   4.

T. re   coo   wa   sin

17 **Find the three words in a row.** Then listen and repeat.
Check your answers. TR: 6.17

1. c as in *cup* or c as in *city*
   at the beginning

2. c as in *face*, k or x
   at the end

18 **Listen.** Then listen and chant. TR: 6.18

Come on, girls,
Come on, boys.
Clap your hands
and make some noise!

Cake and ice cream, c c c.
A pretty pink kite, k k k.
A nice red bicycle, c c c.
A T. rex in a box, x x x.

Come on, girls,
Come on, boys.
Clap your hands
and make some noise!

19 **Listen.** Then listen and repeat. TR: 6.19 and 6.20

Max Flies a Kite

Max doesn't want to colour the cat. He's looking in his toy box.

He doesn't want his pink cars or his T. rex. He likes his kite.

Max is running in circles near the fence. He can't fly his kite.

Look! Max is racing with the kite on his bicycle! Good idea, Max!

20 **Which sound can you hear?** Listen and (circle).
Then go to page 79. TR: 6.21

1 c as in *colour*	**2** c as in *cup*	**3** x	**4** k
1 c as in *juice*	**2** c as in *circle*	**3** k	**4** x

Review

__pple

c__p

__gg

b __ d

b __ g

t__p

__p

b __ s

p __ ll

__oghurt

sleep __

__at

__ircle

__ite

boo __

bo __

2 **Choose nine words from page 50.** Write them in the grid in pencil.

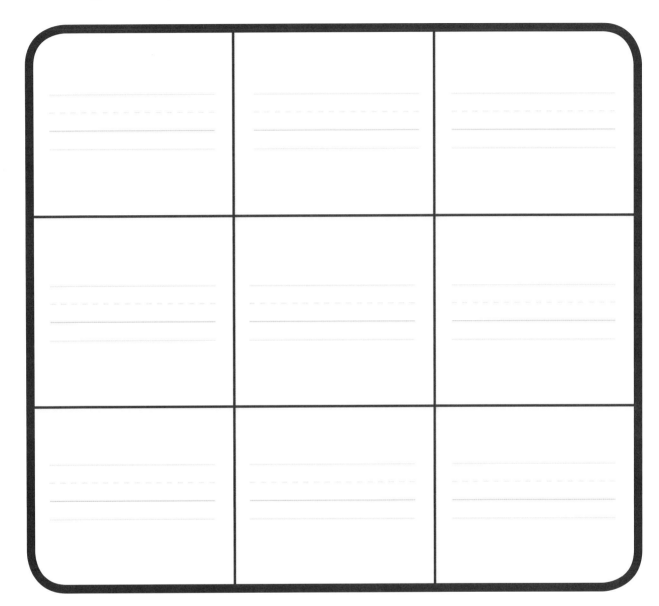

3 **Play *BINGO!*** Tick ✔ the words as you hear them.

1 **Listen.** Then listen and repeat. TR: 7.1 and 7.2

Rr

1.
2.

run   rock

3.
4.
5.

room   robot   rabbit

2 **Trace and say.**

3 **Can you hear r?** Listen and (circle) Yes or No. TR: 7.3

1. Yes No   2. Yes No   3. Yes No   4. Yes No

4 **Can you hear the word with r one or two times?**
Listen and (circle) 1 or 2. TR: 7.4

1.
2.
3.
4.

   1 2   1 2   1 2   1 2

5 **Listen.** Then listen and repeat. TR: 7.5 and 7.6

Hh

1.
h ead

2.
h and

3.
h air

4.
h at

5.
h ippo

6 **Trace and say.**

7 **Can you hear h?** Listen and (circle) Yes or No. TR: 7.7

1. Yes No   2. Yes No   3. Yes No   4. Yes No

8 **Can you hear the word with h one or two times?**
Listen and (circle) 1 or 2. TR: 7.8

1.
1   2

2.
1   2

3.
1   2

4.
1   2

9 **Listen.** Then listen and repeat. TR: 7.9 and 7.10

Gg

1.
gym

2.
giraffe

3.

4.

5.

huge   page   orange

10 **Trace and say.**

11 **Is g at the beginning or at the end?** Listen and repeat. Tick. ✔ TR: 7.11

1.

2.

3.

4.

○ ● ○   ○ ● ○   ○ ● ○   ○ ● ○

12 **Can you hear g?** Listen and (circle) Yes or No. TR: 7.12

1. Yes No   2. Yes No   3. Yes No   4. Yes No

13 **Listen.** Then listen and repeat. TR: 7.13 and 7.14

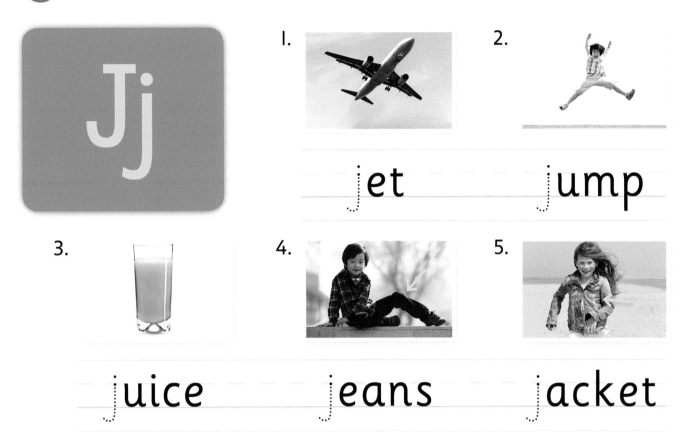

J j

1. jet

2. jump

3. juice

4. jeans

5. jacket

14 **Trace and say.**

15 **Can you hear the word with j one or two times?**
Listen and (circle) I or 2. TR: 7.15

1. I 2

2. I 2

3. I 2

4. I 2

16 **Listen and repeat.** Then write *g* or *j*. TR: 7.16

1. __iraffe 2. __uice 3. oran__e 4. __et

17 **Look, say and circle.** Use red, blue, green and black.

r   h   g   j

18 **Listen.** Then listen and chant. TR: 7.17

Time to move for you and me!
Let's move together I, 2, 3.

R is for run, r r r.
H is for hot, h h h.
G is for gym, g g g.
J is for jump, j j j.

Let's move together I, 2, 3.
This is fun for you and me!

19 **Listen.** Then listen and repeat. TR: 7.18 and 7.19

George's Robot

Jenny jumps with her huge, red jet.

Oh, no! Look at George's robot on the rug!

Jenny puts a hippo head on George's robot.

This is hard!

She puts an orange hand on George's robot.

There. Just right! George!

George runs into the room.

Here's your robot.

My robot!

20 **Which sound can you hear?** Listen and circle. Then go to page 79. TR: 7.20

1 h	2 h	3 r	4 r
1 j	2 g	3 j	4 g

1 **Listen.** Then listen and repeat. TR: 8.1 and 8.2

1.

th̲is

2. that

3.

4.

5.

mother   father   feather

2 **Trace and say.**

3 **Is th at the beginning or in the middle?** Listen and repeat. Tick. ✔ TR: 8.3

1.

2.

3.

4.

○ ○ ◉   ○ ○ ◉   ○ ○ ◉   ○ ○ ◉

4 **Can you hear th?** Listen and ⟨circle⟩ Yes or No. TR: 8.4

1. Yes No   2. Yes No   3. Yes No   4. Yes No

5 **Listen.** Then listen and repeat. TR: 8.5 and 8.6

th

1.
three

2.
thirsty

3.

4.

5.

mouth   teeth   panther

6 **Trace and say.**

7 **Is th at the beginning, in the middle or at the end?**
Listen and repeat. Tick. ✔ TR: 8.7

1.  ◯ ◯ ◯

2.  ◯ ◯ ◯

3.  ◯ ◯ ◯

4.  ◯ ◯ ◯

8 **Can you hear th as in *this* or th as in *thin*?**
Listen and circle. TR: 8.8

1. th th   2. th th   3. th th   4. th th

59

9 **Listen.** Then listen and repeat. TR: 8.9 and 8.10

ch

1.
ch**eese**

2.
ch**icken**

3.

4.

5.

lun**ch**   san**d**wi**ch**   tea**c**her

10 **Trace and say.**

11 **Is ch at the beginning, in the middle or at the end?**
Listen and repeat. Tick. ✓ TR: 8.11

1.  ○ ○ ○

2.  ○ ○ ○

3.  ○ ○ ○

4.  ○ ○ ○

12 **Can you hear ch?** Listen and (circle) *Yes* or *No*. TR: 8.12

1. Yes No   2. Yes No   3. Yes No   4. Yes No

13 **Listen.** Then listen and repeat. TR: 8.13 and 8.14

sh

1.

sh oes

2.

sh irt

3.

fi sh

4.

bu sh

5.

milk sh ake

14 **Trace and say.**

15 **Is sh at the beginning or at the end?** Listen and repeat. Tick. ✓ TR: 8.15

1.

○ ◐ ○

2.

○ ◐ ○

3.

○ ◐ ○

4.

○ ◐ ○

16 **Can you hear ch or sh?** Listen and write *ch* or *sh*. TR: 8.16

1. __ __op 2. wat __ __ 3. __ __elf 4. ben __ __

17 **Follow the path to the pictures with the same sound.**

18 **Listen.** Then listen and chant. TR: 8.17

Time to chant for you and me!
Let's chant together 1, 2, 3.

Mother makes smoothies, th th th.
For three thirsty children, th th th.
Choose peach or cherry, ch ch ch.
Wash our T-shirts, Mummy, sh sh sh.

Let's chant together 1, 2, 3.
This is fun for you and me!

19 **Listen.** Then listen and repeat. TR: 8.18 and 8.19

Theo's Birthday

Theo, Alisha and their mother and father are at the beach. It's Theo's birthday.

There are cheese sandwiches and chocolate milkshakes with cherries on top.

They run to their grandmother and grandfather on the path. Oh, no! Look at their lunch!

Hi!

The raccoons finish and run into the bushes.

It's OK. There's a birthday cake for lunch! Make a wish, Theo!

20 **Which sound can you hear?** Listen and circle.
Then go to page 79. TR: 8.20

| 1 **th** as in *this* | 2 **th** as in *three* | 3 ch | 4 ch |
| 1 ch | 2 sh | 3 sh | 4 sh |

1 **Listen.** Then listen and repeat. TR: 9.1 and 9.2

Ww

1.

2.

worm   watch

3.

4.

5.

walrus   water   woman

2 **Trace and say.**

3 **Can you hear w?** Listen and ⟨circle⟩ Yes or No. TR: 9.3

1. Yes No   2. Yes No   3. Yes No   4. Yes No

4 **Can you hear the word with w one or two times?**
Listen and ⟨circle⟩ 1 or 2. TR: 9.4

1.

2.

3.

4.

1 2   1 2   1 2   1 2

5 **Listen.** Then listen and repeat. TR: 9.5 and 9.6

1.
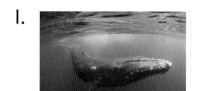

2.

whale   **wh**ite

3.

4.

5.

wheel   **wh**isper   **wh**iskers

6 **Trace and say.**

7 **Can you hear wh?** Listen and (circle) *Yes* or *No.* TR: 9.7

1. Yes No   2. Yes No   3. Yes No   4. Yes No

8 **Can you hear the word with wh one or two times?**
Listen and (circle) *1* or *2.* TR: 9.8

1.

2.

3.

4.

1   2   1   2   1   2   1   2

9 **Listen.** Then listen and repeat. **TR: 9.9 and 9.10**

ng

1.

2.

wing   sing

3.

4.

5.

hang   flying   running

10 **Trace and say.**

11 **Can you hear ng?** Listen and (circle) *Yes* or *No.* **TR: 9.11**

1. Yes No   2. Yes No   3. Yes No   4. Yes No

12 **Can you hear the word with ng one or two times?**
Listen and (circle) *I* or *2.* **TR: 9.12**

1.

2.

3.

4.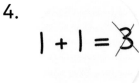

I   2   I   2   I   2   I   2

13 **Listen.** Then listen and repeat. TR: 9.13 and 9.14

mb

1.

cli**mb**

2.

la**mb**

3.

thu**mb**

4.

co**mb**

5.

to**mb**

14 **Trace and say.**

15 **Can you hear mb?** Listen and (circle) *Yes* or *No*. TR: 9.15

1. Yes No   2. Yes No   3. Yes No   4. Yes No

16 **Can you hear ng or mb?** Listen and write *ng* or *mb*. TR: 9.16

1.

lo__ __

2.

stro__ __

3.

cru__ __s

4.

swi__ __

17 **Find the three words in a row.** Then listen and repeat. Check your answers. TR: 9.17

1. wh, ng or mb at the beginning or at the end

2. w, ng or mb at the beginning or at the end

18 **Listen.** Then listen and chant. TR: 9.18

Time to chant for you and me!
Let's chant together 1, 2, 3.

A worm in the weeds, w w w.
Where's the white whale, wh wh wh?
Flying birds singing, ng ng ng.
Little lambs climbing, mb mb mb.

Let's chant together 1, 2, 3.
This is fun for you and me!

19 **Listen.** Then listen and repeat. TR: 9.19 and 9.20

Wendy and Little Lamb

Wendy Wang is calling her white cat. His name is Little Lamb.

Come inside, Little Lamb!

Why don't you climb, Little Lamb?

Little Lamb isn't listening.

Wendy is moving a mouse on a string, but Little Lamb doesn't want to play.

Here, Little Lamb!

What are you doing?

Look at Little Lamb! *Now* he wants to play!

20 **Which sound can you hear?** Listen and ⊙circle.
Then go to page 80. TR: 9.21

1 wh	**3** wh	**5** ng	**7** ng
1 ng	**3** mb	**5** w	**7** mb

Start

___ock

___eese

la_____

mo_____er

_____oes

_____

flyi_____

Move forwards I space.

mou_____

_____

ch   sh   w   wh   ng   mb

Move
back
I space.

Finish

fea___er

___ite

___at

lun___

___ree

oran___e

1 **Work in pairs.** Write the letters or words.

2 **Play the game.** Say the letter, sound and word.

r r rock

71

Picture Dictionary

1   p   b   t   d

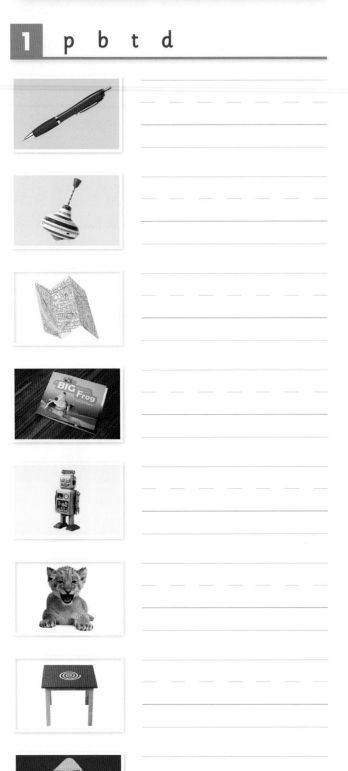

2   s   z   m   n

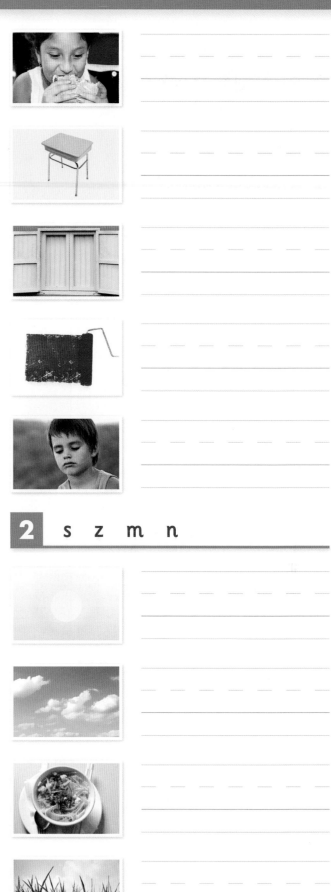

Name: _____
Date: _____

1. 2 + 2 = _____
2. 3 + 1 = _____
3. 2 + 1 =

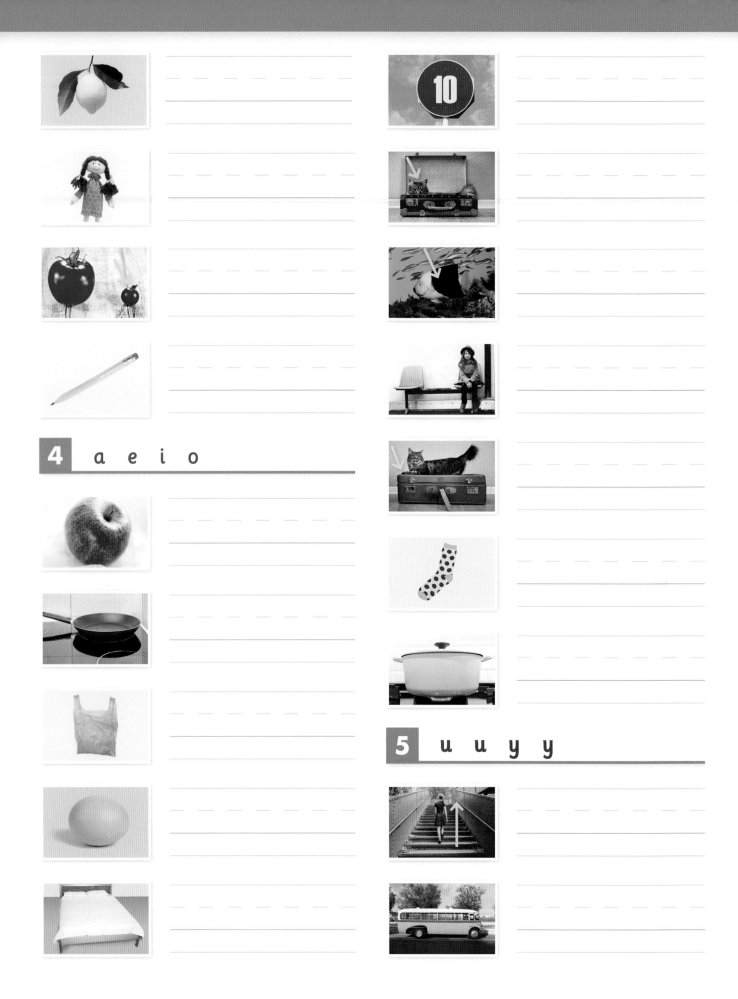

4 a e i o

5 u u y y

7   r   h   g   j

8   th   th   ch   sh

9 | w   wh   ng   mb

Write the numbers from Activity 20. Colour. Write and say.

Unit 1 Use with Activity 20 on page 17.

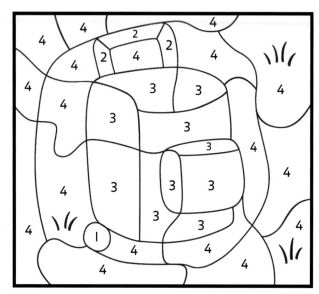

__ag

Unit 2 Use with Activity 20 on page 23.

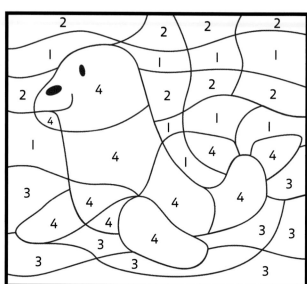

__eal

Unit 3 Use with Activity 20 on page 29.

__eese

Unit 4 Use with Activity 20 on page 37.

d__g

Write the numbers from Activity 20. Colour. Write and say.

Unit 5 Use with Activity 20 on page 43.

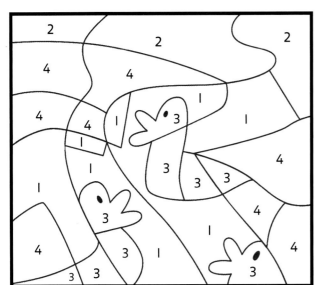

d__cks

Unit 6 Use with Activity 20 on page 49.

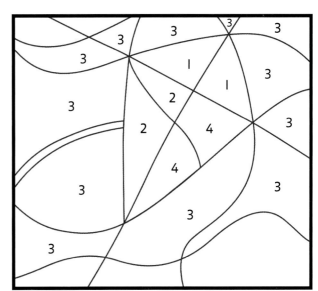

__ite

Unit 7 Use with Activity 20 on page 57.

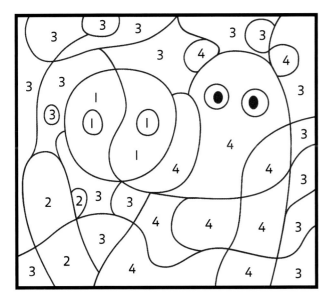

__ippo

Unit 8 Use with Activity 20 on page 63.

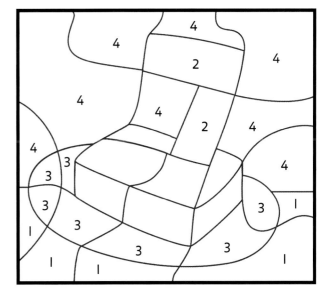

bir__day

Write the numbers from Activity 20. Colour. Write and say.

Unit 9 Use with Activity 20 on page 69.

2 ☐ ☐ ☐ 6 8 ☐ 4

__endy __a__ and
Little La___